DECODING JOY

C. L. FAILS

OTHER TITLES BY C. L. FAILS

The Christmas Cookie Series
The Secret World of Raine the Brain Series
The Ella Books Series
The Sugarplum Universe Books
So Okay...:Treasured Stories from the Life of
James M. Robinson Sr.
My Magical Story Journal

DECODING

JOY

CREATING SPACE & GRACE
TO GROW HOPE

C. L. FAILS

LaunchCrate Publishing

Kansas City, KS

Decoding Joy:
Creating Space & Grace to Grow to Happiness Through Hope

Written by C. L. Fails
Author Headshots by CopperKey Studios
Cover Design by C. L. Fails for LaunchCrate Publishing

© 2022 C. L. Fails

LaunchCrate Publishing
Kansas City, KS
info@launchcrate.com
www.launchcrate.com

Ordering Information:
Quantity sales. Special discounts are available on quantity purchases by corporations, associations, and others. For details, contact the publisher at the email address above. Orders by U.S. trade bookstores and wholesalers.

Library of Congress Control Number: 2022911717

Hardcover ISBN: 978-1-947506-35-0

Printed in the United States of America
10 9 8 7 6 5 4 3 2 1

First Edition

This book is dedicated to the joy seekers.

May you find it.

May you nurture it.

May you share it with others.

FOREWORD

C.L. *never* fails...

That phrase enters my mind every time I read her name. Witnessing her outstanding displays of courage, fortitude, resilience, execution, and creativity through a myriad of experiences has proven it true over and over again. She is someone worth taking the time to hear from.

You'll learn how we first met later in this book, so I'll leave you to read that then. But what I will say is that, even though we've known each other a relatively short amount of time,

Joy is really one of those...mysterious and elusive aspects of life that evades us on a regular basis.

almost 3 years at the time of writing this, she has quickly become a prominent figure in my life and work - and one of my most trustworthy and dependable friends.

She lives from the heart. She laughs - a lot. She dances and eats oatmeal. She's a weird and wise soul. Tune in to what she shares. She has tapped into something deep and special in the human experience and creates ripple effects of goodness that are sure to outlive her.

She also has impressively penned over a dozen books before the one you're about to read now, yet this one may be the most important so far. What you have in your hands with this book will be part of that legacy.

At first thought, you might think a book about learning how to be joyful seems somewhat unnecessary. I mean, isn't joy a natural part of human life? Well, yes... AND... no.

Joy is really one of those often-assumed-to-be-easily-understood but actually mysterious and elusive aspects of life that evades us on a regular basis. "Decoding Joy," is C.L's survey and heartfelt analysis of her own experiences which unpacks the algorithm of how to reveal it and recreate it in your own life.

Take to heart everything you are about to read. You're in good hands.

Don Carter,
Transformational Coach

CONTENTS

NOTE TO THE READER I.

INTRODUCTION III.

01 THE COOL KIDS 1

02 WHAT IS JOY? 9

03 THE OTHER SIDE OF JOY 15

04 TO REALLY KNOW JOY 23

05 SHIFTING GEARS 35

06 THE JOY MACHINE 53

07 TAKING STOCK OF WHAT IS 67

08 MANIFESTING JOY 81

09 NOW WHAT 91

BONUS: JOYSPIRATION 97

A NOTE TO
THE READER

Hi there! I'm so excited that you've picked up this book. Yes, I know it's not very thick. But, wouldn't that feel pretty daunting - a book on decoding joy that's as hefty as War & Peace? So maybe it doesn't have to be *that* large, but maybe decoding joy is more simplistic than we think.

This isn't the first book on joy, and it certainly won't be the

MAYBE DECODING JOY IS MORE SIMPLISTIC THAN WE THINK.

last. That's not my goal. My hope for this title is that it be a small, mighty, powerful addition to all of the current books that serve to teach us more about joy; what it is, how it works, and how to make it work for you.

My hope for you, joy seeker, is that this book encourages you not only to find the joy within you, but also to create a space for it to live and thrive. Additionally, my hope is that you also

begin to share your joy with others. The world needs more light.

Space and grace,
C. L.

INTRODUCTION

So you're reading a book on Joy…

Yay!

You might be wondering who I am to be writing a book about this topic. Well, like you, I'm someone who's known joy in my life and lost it, before regaining it again. My guess is that's what you're aiming for, getting it back or finding it.

It should be noted that I outlined this book a full year before I actually sat down to write it. I started taking my joy back in

I WOKE UP ONE DAY AND REALIZED I WAS GIVING MY JOY AWAY TO OTHERS AND NOT KEEPING ANY…

the middle of a pandemic (I know y'all!), when I woke up one day and realized I was giving it away to other people and not keeping any for myself. Like, what? Who does that?

Me! And I bet you've done it before too. Sometimes we get so excited about the ability to help others, that we overextend ourselves without realizing it. Then, as part of that overextension, we unknowingly set new norms about

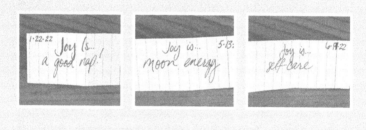

what's acceptable. We're effectively teaching people how to treat us. I did it. I taught someone that they could steal my joy. I taught myself that someone could steal my joy. I taught a whole bunch of someones that my joy was theirs to have and to hold. The truth is, none of that was true. I mean, it was true in the sense that it happened. But it was a false belief I held within the confines of my own mind.

I could give it away and relinquish it, but they couldn't take it

I TAUGHT A WHOLE BUNCH OF SOMEONES
THAT MY JOY WAS THEIRS
TO HAVE AND TO HOLD.

from me. Once I realized this, I started (to borrow the phrase from congress - okay, really just Auntie Maxine) reclaiming my time. My joy was mine to keep or to give away. It was also mine to find. This was in 2020, the year we were all geeked about 20/20 vision and seeing clearly. Well, we got it, didn't we? I'm actually okay with it. My vision is crystal clear now thanks to some coaching, good friends, family support, a bit of therapy, some self-reflection and lots of driving. So much driving! It all sparked a return trip to who I am and what brings me joy.

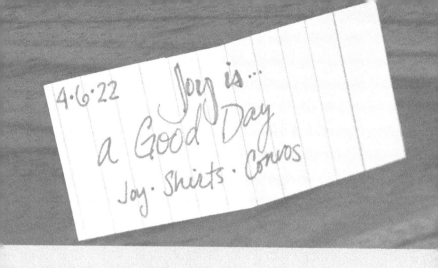

4·6·22

Joy is...
a Good Day
Joy · Shirts · Convos

FINDING JOY DURING OVERWHELM MIGHT SEEM LIKE A PIPE DREAM.

But remember I said I didn't sit down to write this book until a year after I outlined it? Yeah, about that part. I entered 2021 with my intentions set. I was ready to go, and then life came in doing what life does. We all thought 2021 was some sort of scrub relief pitcher that was going to give us a chance to get on base and score some runs against life, which felt like it had a 10 run lead on all of us after 2020. But noooo, 2021 came in hot. Curveballs and sliders. Breaking balls and fastballs. Changeups too. We couldn't do anything with the pitches 2021 was serving up.

Covid mutated the way viruses do for their own survival. Side note: if anything knows about how nothing can steal its joy, it's The Rona. We've lost countless friends and family members to it, and because we're so focused on making (or "not making") things political, the value of human life took a backseat - just the type of joy that The Rona seems to thrive on.

Anyway, Covid mutated several times over. I lost two grandfathers within two months time. My marriage was hanging on by a thread. Business was backed up because I was overwhelmed with and navigating through my own grief journey. Of the top five most stressful life events (death of a loved one, divorce, moving, major illness/injury, work), I was facing or navigating through four of them...in the same year - before the first 6 months had passed. *Insert your

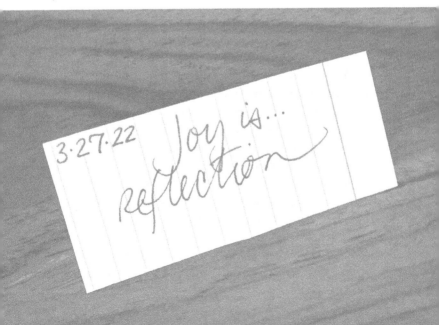

3.27.22 Joy is... Reflection

favorite gif here*

Finding joy during so many overwhelming things, might seem like a pipe dream. And yet, as it stands - 2021 was also one of the most joyous years of my life. I wrote and arranged a 12 track album, ran a ridiculously challenging 5K, and 3 - 10K races (READ: before this year I'd never run more than a 5K and that was in Spring of 2019 [BC - before covid]). Two of those 10K races were in the same month. Color me both surprised and joyous. Seriously, here's something you can color if it brings you joy.

There were so many ups and downs in that year, that it was hard to keep up with all of them. But the truth is, finding joy helped me through grief and standing firm in who I am - and who I'm growing into, and both of those things led me to take some chances in business that helped me to expand my reach.

I was honored with business accolades and connected with

students of all ages about their writing journeys. I even got to be a presenting speaker and a panelist at an International Publishing Summit. I published books by some amazing authors, and was granted grace by other authors all in the same breath. I published the final novel in a romance trilogy that I penned, and released an audiobook version of the first in the series on the same day.

I'm still a bit behind on business as I sit on my living room couch to write this introduction on this cold and gray January day (that followed on the heels of a 60 degree day - because midwest weather's gonna do what midwest weather's gonna do) but I have a plan and am taking steps to get back on track. I'm staring at the Joy Jar that's hanging out on the fireplace mantle and looking at all of the slips of paper that currently fill it. I've managed to keep up with

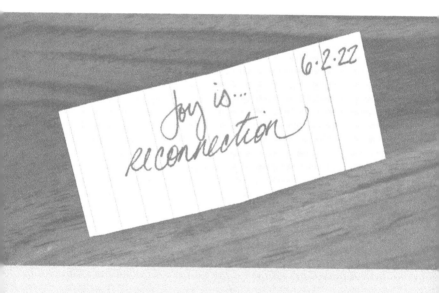

JOY IS A DEEP-ROOTED HAPPINESS THAT'S HANGING OUT BEHIND ALL WE'VE CRAMMED IN FRONT OF IT.

19 days of the year thus far. It's working because I have a plan for tracking it - my Joy. See, you have to be intentional about it. Sometimes it can find you, but you have to seek it out as well.

Yes. Joy can come to us in spontaneous and random moments of bliss. But so often joy resides in the shadows of seemingly the mundane. Acknowledging those moments for what they are is an intentional step in maintaining joy during a pandemic that has senselessly morphed into an endemic. And, my guess is that they'll work beyond that too if you're open to it.

There are so many people in my life who helped me find my joy, and I love them all to the moon and back. Without them, I know this journey would have been so much more

difficult. But with them in my corner, cheering me on and quietly (and sometimes not so quietly) championing me as a human being - not in my role as daughter, granddaughter, sister, aunt, wife, friend, cousin, niece, publisher, writer, illustrator, board member, etc. - seeing me for who I am and sitting with me in my humanity, helped to keep things in perspective for me.

So, if you're ready to learn more about my journey and use it as a spark to create a roadmap to find your own joy, you're in the right place. A small warning first, don't let my humorous take get in the way of your journey. I hope instead that it propels you to a place of finding joy in the smallest nooks and crannies of your own life. That's a funny word, crannies. Does anybody use it without the word nooks? Let's try it.

Joy can be found in the crannies of your heart and mind. Meh - let's keep them together.

Anyway, Joy is a deep-rooted happiness that's hanging out behind all the stuff that life has crammed in front of it. Correction, it's hanging out behind all the life stuff that we crammed in front of it. So let's go rummaging around through all the extra things we're carrying to find some joy. I think it's time for a yard sale anyway.

CHAPTER ONE
THE COOL KIDS

To know joy, true joy, there must be a deep appreciation for the balance in which that joy can exist. It's quite the conundrum when you think about it. To know joy, I have to have an understanding of that thing we often spend much of our lives attempting to avoid. Phew! But when we hold space for each other, when we allow each other to experience all the feels and are present with them through all of it, we, the

TO KNOW JOY THERE MUST BE AN APPRECIATION FOR THE BALANCE IN WHICH IT CAN EXIST.

cool kids, are actually helping to foster joy.

I recently went rollerskating with my Godson. It was noon on a Thursday, in the summertime. Why are these things important? Well, you can guess the type of crowd that was all laced up and ready to skate. We were the 5th and 6th people to enter the rink on that day and I watched as it began to fill with elementary aged children and the adults

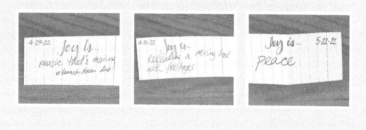

who brought them there on that day. There were those who already had a basic handle on how to stay upright on those 8 wheels, and there were those who were learning and using a skate buddy to do so. If you haven't been introduced to a skate buddy yet, let me paint a picture for you.

Imagine the nearly triangle roof of Snoopy's house, flipped on its side. Add wheels to the bottom of it and you have the basic shape of a skate buddy. It's basically a PVC walker

WHEN WE HOLD SPACE FOR EACH OTHER, WE ARE HELPING TO FOSTER JOY.

with small skate wheels. Anywho, the rink was full of little ones and their skate buddies.

Thing is, there's no skate buddy lane in this rink. They're basically rolled out there onto the floor and asked to figure it out, which is exactly what they were doing. They were all over the place, falling and getting back up, cutting corners wide and tight. Skating serpentine because they're following whichever direction the skate buddy goes. It was fun to watch but a bit challenging to skate around at times,

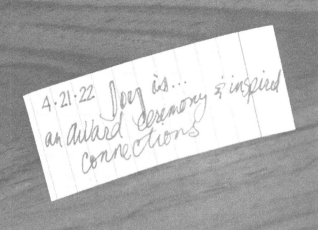

4.21.22 Joy is...
an award ceremony & inspired
connections

HUMANITY AT ITS FINEST: THOSE WHO COULD, HELPING THOSE WHO WERE TRYING.

especially when they and their skate buddies started skating in packs.

Imagine it, gangs of 1st, 2nd and 3rd graders trying to learn how to roller skate and terrorizing the rink in flocks of 10. Everybody's skating all willy nilly, and every 3rd person falls down without prompting. Bodies on the floor and skate buddies pushed ahead, propelled proportionately with the momentum of the drop. It was mass chaos but what I witnessed and got to actively participate in was a perfect example of what we've been discussing in this chapter.

A bunch of Cool Kids, who could skate, would willingly and without prompting stop to help up those who were learning. They'd ask if they were okay, go get, return, then hold the skate buddy so the skater could steady themselves as they returned to a wobbly legged stance on their skates. It was humanity at its finest, honestly. Those who could, helping those who were trying. There was no judgment, no laughing, and they were actively helping to bring joy to those who kept falling. The smiles on the faces of those who had fallen returned every single time without fail, because they were skating again. The Cool Kids were crucial to the experience of those who were learning. Imagine the scene playing out differently.

You're learning how to skate and you're watching kids who might be the same age as you, skating without the plastic walker. You're feeling unstable, your legs knocking like a baby deer learning to walk. You begin to compare yourself to those around you - yikes! This could be a whole chapter in and of itself. Maybe I'll do that. Anyway, you're tremendously nervous and are trying to get it together when you fall.

Now imagine those same skaters, gliding by and laughing, not stopping to help, making jokes at your expense. This is what we're likely conditioned to expect from people in American culture. Yes, even children. They're learning it from somewhere, right? From the floor, attempting to get back up

after you've fallen, and watching people laugh at you...how much would you enjoy skating after an experience like that? How likely would you be to find joy in that experience? But the inverse encourages it.

It didn't matter if they fell or were unsure of themselves, they rolled right out to join the line for limbo or the dice game. The Cool Kids encouraged that. They set the scene, created the environment for joy to exist in a space where it might otherwise not. And for those who needed the skate buddies, because they understood what it was like to fall, they had a greater appreciation for being upright and skating beside

THEY SET THE SCENE, CREATED THE ENVIRONMENT FOR JOY TO EXIST IN A SPACE WHERE IT MIGHT OTHERWISE NOT.

those who were able to skate without the aid of the walker on wheels. Each skater got increasingly better throughout the two hours we were there. Every single one of them.

And, when I couldn't successfully get out of the way of one of the fallen and I ended up kissing the rink floor myself, they stopped skating long enough to ask if I was okay, even those with skate buddies.

What a dope example of humanity and the importance of being a true Cool Kid within the communities in which you live and thrive. It's likely one I won't soon forget as I have a new strawberry on my knee to remind me. I kid, but I am truly grateful to have experienced it.

Hey Cool Kid! Here's to holding space for others on this journey, and fostering a space for joy to thrive. Let's set an intention to build the type of environment around us that would help us feel more confident with our own metaphorical skate buddies. Your intention, your desire, will set a foundation for all that comes as you begin decoding joy.

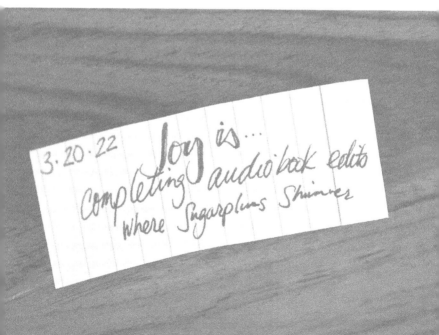

CHAPTER TWO
WHAT IS JOY?

According to the dictionary, Joy is a feeling of great pleasure and happiness: *tears of joy | the joy of being alive.* Synonyms of joy are plentiful. My favorites of the bunch: delight, great pleasure, jubilation, triumph, exultation, gladness, glee, exhilaration, ebullience, exuberance, elation, euphoria, bliss, ecstasy, radiance, enjoyment, gratification, and last but certainly not least, felicity.

JOY IS SOMETHING MUCH DEEPER THAN HAPPINESS.

I often see joy and happiness used interchangeably, but this list of synonyms shows joy to be something much deeper than happiness. I mean, felicity alone is defined as intense happiness. That tells me on the scale of emotions, joy far surpasses happiness. So we know it's more profound than happiness, but what is joy and where does it come from?

Let's start with the latter part of that question.

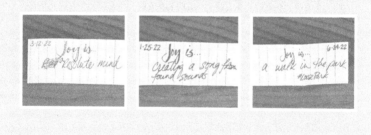

Joy requires surrender in order to experience its fullness and complete potential.

Joy is a choice. When that choice becomes a habit, it fundamentally shifts how you see the world, which changes how you show up in the world.

What we believe, drives our actions, which impacts our results, which reinforces what we believe. If I seek out the

JOY REQUIRES SURRENDER IN ORDER TO EXPERIENCE ITS FULLNESS.

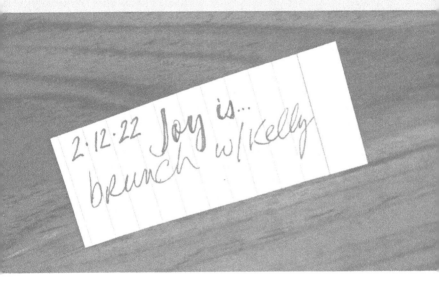

2·12·22 Joy is... brunch w/Kelly

joy that exists within a day, what I typically find is that I have a hard time figuring out which joy to document. When I'm having an off day and I look at all of the hard things going on around me, I find more things that are also challenging and finding that one joyous thing (whether internal or external) becomes much harder to identify. This is the paradox of choosing joy. You must actively pursue it, or it almost becomes an elusive pursuit; something that I almost experienced but it was just out of reach, something I see others enjoying, but not me. Then joy becomes something

4·20·22 Joy is·:·
early morning collabs

JOY IS A CHOICE.

I'm just not supposed to have. It becomes something that's great for everyone else, but not for me. That in turn, makes it something I secretly want, but feel like I can't have, which brings up feelings of envy, misery, grief or sorrow, which are all the opposite of what we really want. Joy.

Now you're thinking, "so you're telling me I have to surrender to feel joy?" Yes. I am. But the beautiful thing about it, once you finally let go - and I do mean let go...even of that tiny little piece of thread that makes you feel like you still have some control even though it would likely snap under the weight of anything treacherous - there is abundant joy. Let's try something.

Think about the one thing that brings you the most joy in the world. The one thing you wouldn't give up, even for a million dollars. Got it? Great!

Now imagine that thing and feel the joy it brings you. Let that joy cover you. Are you smiling? You should be. If you're not - keep thinking about it until you do. That thing has brought enough joy to your soul to physically change your body. You love it so much that you hold it in the palm of your hand and hold it tight because you don't want to lose it. Without realizing it, two things are happening as you do this.

One, that thing you love - not only can you not see it, but it's now being suffocated. You're squeezing the life and joy right out of it. It might even be changing shape under the pressure of your hand, which fundamentally changes it into something different from what you were initially trying to protect. Open that palm up and now it's crushed joy. Deflated. No longer likely to bring you anything except despair or anguish.

 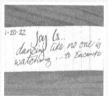 

Two, that thing that you love is likely not the only one of its kind. But nothing else can enter your hand. You're holding on so tight to that one thing that gives you joy, that you're missing out on some other things that exist that can also bring you joy.

So yes. Let go. Surrender. Allow things to be, as they are in their own form. Open your palms to the sun and welcome in light. Joy is waiting on you.

CHAPTER THREE
THE OTHER SIDE OF JOY

So we're talking about what joy is. But what's on the other side of it? Antonyms of joy are misery and despair. I spent a bit of time there in my life.

Once I graduated from high school and moved on to college,

MISERY SEEMED TO COVER ME
LIKE A BLANKET.

my entry into the pursuit of the American Dream had begun. You know the dream; pursue a solid career - meet the love of your life - buy a house - start a family - raise said family - work, work, work - retire. I was on the journey to pursuing a solid career. The only problem? I had no earthly idea what career I wanted to pursue.

I remember watching my parents drive away after helping

me move into West Hall on the campus of Kansas State University, and thinking to myself, "now what?"

That summer I had attended orientation and enrolled in classes (including Calculus 1 - which apparently my test scores said I was prepared to handle even though *I* was trying to sign up for College Algebra) before heading back to Kansas City. So my schedule was set, but I hadn't declared a major. There I was, standing in the parking lot with my

THEY WERE EXPERTS IN PURSUIT OF THE AMERICAN DREAM."

brother, watching our parents drive off and feeling a sense of, "Oh shit."

I'm so thankful for my brother. I'm not sure what I would've done next had he not been a student at the same school. My roommate hadn't arrived yet, so he asked if I wanted to hang out at his apartment for a while. It was an offer I gladly accepted.

After a couple of hours of hanging out with my brother and

IMPOSTER SYNDROME SHOWED OUT WHEN IT SHOWED UP.

delaying the inevitable, he drove me back to campus where I got to meet my roommate, Amber, in person. I'm not sure how they matched us so well, but I found myself grateful yet again to have someone who was pretty easy going as a roommate. Within the first month of classes, I knew I was in over my head in that dang math class they said I tested into.

The University called our room and sent emails to me, attempting to connect me to tutoring for the course, all thanks to my Calc Lab instructor who could see me flailing.

I'd struggled through a class before, but I had never flailed quite like I had in that one. It was pretty epic. If I were to take that course today, my 40+ year old brain would probably handle it far better than my 18 year old brain. Why? Because I was overwhelmed with the experience of college and I didn't know it. It's ridiculously easy to see reflecting on it now. But when I was in it, I just felt overwhelmed. Since I hadn't declared a major, I was taking courses in majors that I thought I might want to explore. I was enrolled in a course meant to help you narrow down your field of interest and focus. Instead it brought more confusion.

I was learning how to take care of myself while still trying to figure out how to take care of the work. That first semester was a lot. A lot of overwhelm. A lot of self-convincing. A lot of denial. A lot of internal fear. But not a lot of joy. The second

semester was better, but I still had no clue what I was going to major in and I let that thought hang out rent-free in my head while I was doing my best to improve my GPA that took quite a hit because I hadn't dropped my 5 credit hour Calc course. The truth is, I didn't know what it meant to drop a course. I felt too overwhelmed and ashamed to ask in that first semester. Different story by the time I graduated though. I was a course dropping pro by then. But first semester, and even into my second semester I didn't understand the concept of removing a class from your schedule if you'd already paid for it.

All of that angst, all of the overwhelm led to a sense that I

didn't know what I was doing. I was watching everyone else walk around campus like they had their lives together. They were the experts in pursuit of the American Dream. Having worked with first year students in Higher Ed, looking back on

THINKING ABOUT THE CLIMB UP THE STAIRCASE CAUSED MY CHEST TO GET TIGHT

it, they were likely faking it unlike the rest of us who were okay with the outward displays of confusion and discontent. Imposter Syndrome showed out when it showed up in my life.

By the time I reached the Fall semester of my second year in college, I was totally overwhelmed with life. I often describe that window of time to people as a sense of being on the floor level of a dry well that has a narrow spiral staircase available to lead you back to the ground surface. To look up

I WAS ON THE OTHER SIDE OF JOY...AND I STAYED THERE FOR QUITE SOME TIME.

at the staircase meant I'd have to strain my neck because it extended that steep and high into the air.

I knew I needed to get out of the well, but the climb up the staircase, just like the thought of staying on campus for another semester, cause my chest to feel tight.

Misery and despair seemed to cover me like a blanket. I was on the other side of joy in that moment, and I stayed there for quite some time.

CHAPTER FOUR
TO REALLY KNOW JOY

Well that last chapter was tough, but one that's important to understand when attempting to decode joy. Keep reading and it will all make sense. I promise.

I'm looking out my front window right now, thinking about

THE REASON I KNOW JOY SO WELL
IS BECAUSE I ALSO KNOW SADNESS.

life and all of its mystery, and it strikes me. The reason I know joy so well is because I also know sadness. I embrace it. I feel it. I don't wallow in it. But I feel it. And because I allow it to do its work within me, I'm truly able to appreciate when things are joyous.

I can vividly remember moments from childhood where I was sad about something and some adult tried to encourage

 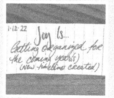 

me to feel better. It was the other children, my classmates, who would sit with me in sadness until it passed. It's in us to empathize with each other, but our culture somehow teaches us to lock up those melancholy thoughts quick, fast, and in a hurry, and put a smile on your face. But that's just not how we're wired to work as humans. Do you know how I know this? All you have to do is watch how babies and toddlers react to music or sadness in others.

BECAUSE I ALLOW IT TO DO ITS WORK WITHIN ME, I'M TRULY ABLE TO APPRECIATE WHEN THINGS ARE JOYOUS.

In 2009, before my niece turned one, my then fiancé's father unexpectedly passed away. My family gathered at my parents' house to sit with him as we figured out next steps to get him home with his immediate family. When my brother, sister-in-law, and niece arrived, they all hugged him. My niece though, knew something wasn't right. She looked him in his eyes and patted his face, then leaned in to hug him and patted his back - her tiny fingers drumming just behind his shoulder, as if to let him know that whatever it was he was feeling was going to be okay. That isn't unique

I DON'T WALK AROUND HAPPY ALL THE TIME,
BUT I STILL KNOW DEEP JOY.

to her. That's human nature - if we encourage instead of stifle it. Think about that for a moment. When babies cry, we try to figure out what they need - is it hunger, a dirty diaper, do they just need connection? Sometimes when we're exhausted and overwhelmed we may want them to just stop crying, but generally speaking, we try to assess what they need.

It's intrinsically in us to support each other, but we condition it right on out of each other.

At my high school graduation, way back in the late 1900s, our class was lined up two by two, to march into the auditorium and one of the coaches was so proud of me that he hugged me and followed it with a kiss - on the lips, which threw me completely off kilter. As it should have. I looked at one of my classmates in confusion. He looked on in horror and shock. I was angry and embarrassed and my eyebrows began to furrow as I was now forced to process something that happened in a split second, but clearly left a lasting impact on me because here I am writing about it more than two decades after it happened. Our parallel lines began to move much faster towards the auditorium opening and we could now see the friends and family who came to cheer on our accomplishments. Can you imagine it? In what was supposed to be one of the most joyous moments in life, according to what our society tells us anyway, there I was

trying to quickly process something I didn't ask for, nor want, so I could enjoy the celebration of what I'd been working towards since I was 5 years old. Before I could work through it myself, I heard a man blurt out, "SMILE hunny! This is a happy occasion!"

SHEESH!! In less than a two minute window, I had a glimpse of the unwanted side of being a woman in America and I didn't even know it. Thankfully I didn't allow that to color the lens through which I saw the world, but it would have been easy enough to do had there not been other men present in the moment that offered a counter micro experience that unknowingly helped to affirm that what I was feeling, as I was processing it, was okay.

I looked up in the direction of the voice to see who they were talking to. I can still describe in detail what this older white man was wearing, his white polo shirt and khaki pants, his graying and thinning hair and his salt and pepper facial hair. He made eye contact with me and nodded. He clearly had no idea what I'd just experienced, but the thought that I was anything but happy in that moment was too much for him to comprehend. I looked back at my classmate and he gazed at me with apologetic eyes - the micro experience.

What if I was feeling melancholy about the uncertainty that was on the other side of graduation? What if I was ruminating about my friend who was on her way to the Air Force the next day? What if I was reminiscing on all of the good moments

I'd had with the humans who were - at that very moment - filing into the auditorium like animals into Noah's Ark? What if I was processing all of these at the same time and I started to tear up as a result of the beauty that I'd found within my awkward high school experience? Who was this Gap Daddy to tell me how to display my emotions - even if I hadn't just been accosted by a teacher?

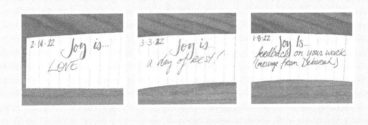

I still found joy in the moment, in my own way. It was filtered through a melancholy and bittersweet lens, but it was still joy. It may not have looked like the sappy and sanguine joy that we expect to see, but I still felt deep happiness and a fullness that was hard to describe. It was hanging out in there amongst all the other emotions I was experiencing. Speaking of, I think we sometimes forget how complex our emotions can be, and just how sophisticated our bodies are at feeling multiple things at once.

In the last chapter I talked about my first semester of college and how I found myself feeling overwhelmed with a lot of things - classes, not feeling like I knew what I was doing, finding a place or group where I fit in. It all piled up and felt too big to handle. I came home from class one day, dropped the Boyz II Men Evolution cd in my stereo and skipped to track 2. "Never." I let it play, on repeat, for at least four hours (though I'm almost certain it was more like four days) when Amber, my roommate, finally couldn't take it anymore and snapped. "Can we listen to something happy?!" The truth is, though the music itself was melancholy, the lyrics of the song were not. They were encouraging, just like the micro experience I'd had in high school, and later, like the micro experience I'd had in watching my niece comfort my grieving fiancé. That song allowed me to feel all the feels in a way that helped me remember that it was human to

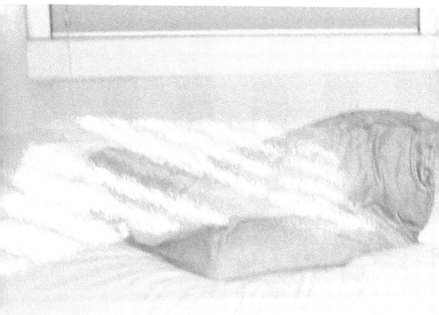

experience anxiety, awkwardness, confusion, fear, nostalgia, sadness - all the things, and navigate through it. There was a gentleness that I found within that song that comforted me through the uncertainty in a way that still honored my experience. It didn't ask me to shut out the hard stuff. Instead it encouraged me to not allow the hard stuff to get in the way of embracing the good stuff that was yet to come. I'd like to thank Babyface for reinforcing that internal shift.

Don't get me wrong, I still have to catch myself when I see people cry and when I cry myself. I'm getting out of the habit of telling them (and me), "Don't cry," and shifting instead to holding their hand in silence or encouraging them to "let it out." I started unlearning this as I watched how a good friend would patiently sit with me as I let out years-worth of emotions that I'd been holding in for fear of causing

discomfort to others. There's no joy in that.

Whew! Years and years of throttling my own emotions in multiple areas of my life so I wouldn't offend or upset someone else. Even within my marriage I'd been on the receiving end of similar messages. We're not talking indirect messaging. It was very direct, "You sure know how to make me feel like crap," was the reply I received when I told

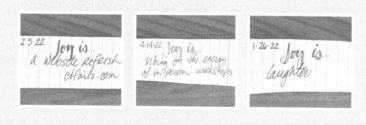

them how it felt to be on the receiving end of an action that belittled me.

Why is this important to know? Why would I share something so deeply personal? Because a large chunk of us have likely allowed something similar in our life at some point in time. On the flip side, at some point in our life we might have also been the one dishing it out. Neither of those positions fosters a place for joy to thrive.

BECAUSE I ALLOW IT TO DO ITS WORK WITHIN ME, I'M TRULY ABLE TO APPRECIATE WHEN THINGS ARE JOYOUS.

Within our society we condition certain populations to take a back seat and in doing so, we also rob them from an opportunity to find true joy. How? When you're constantly in search of external validation that you and/or your experience matters, then you miss the joy that's often right in front of your face. In turn, we often trade that joy for a desperate scramble to outwardly display our importance. The latter is absent of the hope that's needed for joy to blossom.

Because of my own kindness and consideration of others,

and not acknowledging my own needs, I allowed my own emotions and self worth to take a back seat. The scramble. Once I realized what I was doing to myself, I modified my own behavior. I had been so steeped in the idea that being accommodating would allow space for joy when the opposite was true. Setting boundaries creates space for that.

Take note, that's what our society is encouraging when

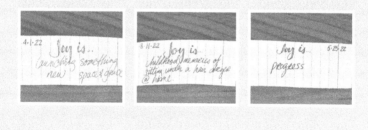

we try to persuade people to "be happy" when they're sad, instead of allowing them to feel what they feel and experience the mystifying duality of the deep joy that comes from also knowing sorrow.

To know joy, true joy, there must be a deep appreciation for the balance in which that joy can exist. I don't walk around happy all the time, but I still know deep joy.

CHAPTER FIVE
SHIFTING GEARS

So I was on the other side of joy through college, when I returned home after my 3rd semester, and after I returned to Kansas State to finish my degree. I'd caught glimpses of Joy when I was working with students as I spent my summers as a Servant Leader within the Kansas City Freedom Schools, but glimpses aren't enough to satiate the spirit.

Eventually I was focused enough to earn my degree in

GLIMPSES OF JOY AREN'T ENOUGH TO
SATIATE THE SPIRIT.

Psychology and I returned to Kansas City, on my quest to fully live the American Dream, without a job, all set to move back in with my parents. Sorry y'all! It was the first Spring semester after September 11th and things were still uncertain and up in the air for a lot of America. There was chatter right before our commencement ceremony about plans post-graduation. There were students who were following up on job offers extended to them after

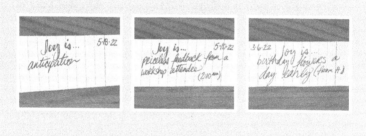

their summer internships pre-9/11. There were a handful more who were off to graduate school because they were struggling to find work at the moment. And even greater was the number of us whose plans included a move to the house of some family member or friend because we were unable to secure work prior to graduation. Living the dream.

I felt fortunate (and still do) to have had a soft place to land after commencement. Not only did I have family support,

I FOUND MYSELF CLOSER TO JOY, BUT NOT QUITE THERE YET.

but their grace also gave me the chance to focus my time on the job hunt. The summer after graduation, I worked with the Kansas City Freedom Schools, but finding work outside of that was beyond challenging. For entry level-positions you needed 2 years of experience. I'm still not sure how you're supposed to gain said experience if it *requires* 2 years of relevant work to get your foot in the door, but that's a topic for another day.

After a year of service with AmeriCorps VISTA, I found my way

I PLOPPED MY EMOTIONAL FLOTATION DEVICES ONTO MY ARMS AND RELAXED INTO THE WAVES OF CHANGE.

to a scholarship program that was willing to bring me on as a Life Coach trainee - I didn't have the experience needed to be a full Life Coach. I was okay with the trainee status because I knew myself. If I could get my foot in the door, I could kick it wide open. And that's exactly what happened. Within this organization I rose from Trainee to Life Coach to co-Director of an initiative for girls, to Assistant Director of Marketing, and by the time I left, I was holding dual roles as Director of Life Skills Curriculum and Instruction, and Director of Marketing.

When I found purpose within my work and my internal chatter shifted back towards words of encouragement, I found myself closer to joy, but not quite there yet. To watch me navigating through my 20s, you could tell I was in search of something that was elusively just outside of my grasp. I didn't know it at the time, but that something was joy. The older I got, the closer to it I became. I found love within, and then found more loving relationships. My brother and sister-in-law expanded their family with a beautiful child, and my capacity for love continued to expand. My life was full of love, happiness and support in spite of the 2008 recession that the country was experiencing. But joy, that slippery elusive son of a gun was still just outside my grasp.

I question now if I ever knew what it was, even when I felt it

as a child. I'm not so sure that understood it for what it was.

In 2009, a new marriage brought its own unique challenges into our lives. The world was continuing to shift and the only way I knew to experience change was to flow with it and not fight it. So I plopped my emotional flotation devices onto my arms and relaxed into the waves of change as they tossed around from one shore to another, as they raged downstream, and as they began to calmly enter a more tranquil state. In 2012 I took a leap of faith, leaving the work I loved and people I loved working with at the scholarship company. I picked up writing and quilting in the 5-month window before I landed at the University of Missouri-Kansas City. Nearly 5 full years after landing in Higher Education I took another leap of faith into the world of publishing, full-time. Along the way, family dynamics and health transformed for a variety of reasons. All the while, I allowed the shifting waters to continue to move me wherever I was being guided. Odd as it may sound, it was both a passive and active journey.

By now I bet you've done the math and you're wondering when I finally got to joy, huh?

Quick answer: October, 2020. That's when a Coaching assignment was given to me. Find the joy.

Somebody right now is thinking, "What? You're telling us it was more than 20 years before you found joy?" Yes. I'm telling you it was more than 20 years before I found joy *and* could identify it as such. There's the difference. Had I experienced deep happiness? Yes. Elation? Yes. Gladness and glee? That sounds like a soul group from the 60's, but yes. Did I know any of those moments as joy? No.

So what was different for me in October of 2020?

Like a lot of us, as we transitioned from the first quarter of

2020 into the month of April, that new quarter brought a lot of uncertainty and stress. Things that were not within my sphere of control were getting amplified on a daily basis and I had begun to allow that accompanying stress to envelop my spirit. I could feel things shifting internally and it didn't feel joyous. In fact, I'd consider it the opposite. I was back on the other side of joy, but this time I had taken off those emotional flotation devices and was actively wading through the change on my own.

I had consistently begun implementing my 3Ps practice to create a sense of routine and normalcy in a world that was anything but. Every morning and evening, I would begin and end my day with a 45 second Plank that shifted into Prayer and meditation in Child's Pose and finished with 20 Push-ups. It was there to help me remain present and in the moment, to feel where I was, physically, emotionally,

SO I LAY THERE...WAITING FOR THE FEELINGS
TO DO WHAT THEY NEEDED TO WITHIN ME.

and mentally, and to remain connected to those I couldn't physically connect with because of the pandemic. I was sharing a 2 bedroom house with my spouse who was also navigating his own way through the new reality delivered to us by the pandemic. The 3Ps were, and still are, my way to create some space to honor my own journey and a much needed reminder of grace that I was doing the best I could in that moment with what I had in front of me. Space & Grace.

I vividly remember a night in April when I entered into the 3P routine that just felt different. I could feel the sorrow welling within my soul and can recall falling into my nightly child's pose and praying for the world at large, a global healing, not just physical bodies but of people's souls that I could seemingly feel sobbing. The tears rolled down my cheeks as my face was buried in the bedroom carpet. I let it out, my own grief, my own hurt, my own sorrow. I didn't want it to take up residence within me. So I lay there, on the floor, forgetting about the push-ups that I hadn't done, waiting

for the feelings to do what they needed to within me. That moment started to awaken a new version of me. Things that I'd been sitting on in the past, I made a commitment to myself to fulfill. When we got out of the pandemic I was going to be a stronger version of myself and I was committed to seeing it through.

Within the publishing company I founded, I had created

a fully fleshed out service to capture family stories and legacies that I wasn't marketing because I had this looming fear that the person whose story I was documenting would have a dog that brought them comfort, and that my fear of dogs would mean I'd ask them to put their pet away, and as a result of that, the dog would be uncomfortable with my presence in the house and would communicate that to their owner, who also wouldn't want me in their house. It was a thoroughly detailed fear that I had allowed to control

THAT WAS WHEN I BEGAN TO FEEL A DEEPER LEVEL OF HOPE.

one of the pieces of my work that could bring a greater amount of joy and hope to those around me. I had allowed my mind to take over and stop the impactful work that had been funneled through me. So in early May, when I realized how ridiculously out of control I had allowed my mind to wander, I took a moment during one of my 3Ps to ask for guidance on how to get over my fear of dogs - a fear I'd carried with me since getting chased home by a doberman daily in 4th grade.

JOY WAS THERE BECAUSE I MADE A
CONSCIOUS DECISION TO ACTIVELY WELCOME
IT IN AMONGST ALL OF THE OTHER EMOTIONS
I WAS FEELING.

As the pandemic rolled on, programming everywhere shifted
to virtual chats and workshops. Not even one week after
asking for guidance on getting through my fear of dogs, I
found myself in a Zoom room serving as a judge for a youth
pitch competition with two other people; one, a friend who
was the reason I signed up for that time slot, and the other,
a Coach who specialized in "helping adults breakthrough
some of the childhood trauma that holds them back on
their personal and professional journey." I wish I could see
the replay of my face the moment he introduced himself.

I wonder if the exterior matched the, "Whaaaaaaaaaaat?!" that was flowing through me internally. Ask and ye shall receive, much? My goodness.

I mentioned to this coach during the judging that I was going to reach out to him about my fear of dogs, *after* there was a team presentation on how to help the increasing dog-shelter population that came as a result of the shifts created by the pandemic - dogs all up and through their presentation. Funny enough, that was the start of where my joy began to shift. That was when I began to feel a deeper level of hope. It was only the very tip of the iceberg, but I can pinpoint where my joy shifted to that very moment. Afterall, joy is the fruit of hope. Where hope is present, it invites a calm that activates joy. Without that moment, my joy journey would have surely taken a detour.

By the end of May, we were tagged in a Facebook post with the other judges and mentors who served during the pitch competition. During my lunch break I was piddling around on my laptop when I saw the post from the organization. I clicked on his name and went to visit his profile - to do a little looky-loo-lurking, you know how you do when you're trying to decide if you want to add someone as a Facebook friend. I was hovering over the friend request button, stalling because I knew in my gut if I was going to overcome this fear, adding him as a friend was likely going to accelerate that process in some way.

Before I could click the trackpad, I received a friend request

 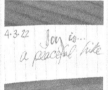 

notification. "No way!" I thought to myself. "It can't be." I had a fleeting thought to take a screenshot of the moment just in case, but curiosity propelled my fingers to act before I stopped to do so. I clicked on the request. Yep. It was from

Coach. I was dumbfounded at the odds of him adding me as a friend at the same moment I was about to add him. I took it as another sign that he was going to help me shift further into the strongest version of myself, so I accepted the request and stayed as open as possible.

By the end of June, I was a coaching client with the premise of addressing my childhood and adulthood fear of dogs. He could see the other layers of grief that I needed to process and shed first, and guided me swiftly through that process in a way that left me feeling empowered to charge forward in both personal and professional growth. By early August, I had begun to regularly apply the work, and when September

MY ACCESS TO JOY SHIFTED FROM PASSIVE TO ACTIVE AND ALMOST MISSION-DRIVEN

arrived, because of the work I'd been putting in within and outside of my sessions, I had created a program to help serve more people who were interested in writing their book. So in October, once the virtual program was rolled out, my coaching sessions shifted to something different. That's when the assignment was given to me - find the joy.

Just 7 days, that's the duration I was encouraged to follow. Each day, I was supposed to find something that brought me joy and go do it. There were no limitations on it. Just, find the joy and live in it. That week because of the internal work I'd been doing, access to joy shifted from something passive to something active - almost mission-driven. I hadn't dropped the ball on one of my assignments yet, and that one, though it felt a bit daunting, I had no desire to drop. Find the joy and check in. I sent an update every day. But more than that, joy became something I was looking forward to experiencing and creating. Joy was now mine to be had. That assignment

was the spark that lit the flame of joy that lives within me right now. I've been stoking that flame for two years; during a pandemic, coming out of it, and navigating the new realities brought with it. Joy has been ever present with me for the last two years. Even through challenges and heartbreak, joy was still there because I made a conscious decision to actively welcome it in amongst all of the other emotions I was feeling.

So the moment my joy shifted was the moment I was open to experiencing something different AND hopeful enough to create it in my own space.

If you were to create A Week of Joy, what would you do? Stay open as you go. Joy comes in many forms and the joy you create may look different from the joy someone else creates. Tag us on your Week of Joy challenge. #weekofjoy #decodingjoy #joychallenge

JOY
CHALLENGE

WEEK OF JOY CHALLENGE

CHAPTER SIX
THE JOY MACHINE

So I found joy again in 2020, and actively held onto it in 2021 and 2022. It's been hanging out with me since the Joy Challenge issued to me in my coaching sessions. Let me add a point of clarity here. There's often a sense that feeling or experiencing joy means you're walking around on cloud nine. But that's not always the case.

JOY ISN'T ALWAYS A FEELING OF EUPHORIA.

Joy isn't always a feeling of euphoria. Joy sometimes slips in during quiet moments and fills your soul with light. That joy, the mouse-whisper version of it, is often the most pure, heartfelt joy that we experience. It's often inexplicable and leaves us in a satiated state of awe and contentment. Here's how quiet joy has shown up for me recently.

It was the day of our Book Fair and 5th Anniversary

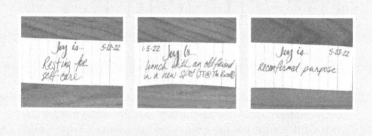

Celebration for LaunchCrate. The weeks leading up to it were full of detail work and planning. I was tired but on a mission to ensure that the authors we support, could feel how much we appreciate them for entrusting us with the telling of their stories, period, but especially on that day. I checked in with all of the authors just before the start of the event, encouraged them to have fun, then slipped away to finish setting up my own table. I smiled inside as I watched the authors begin to introduce themselves to each other and

JOY SOMETIMES SLIPS IN DURING QUIET MOMENTS AND FILLS YOUR SOUL WITH LIGHT.

swap autographed trading cards. There was no prompting from me to do so. They did it on their own with a level of excitement that added to the electricity in the room.

At one moment during the event, the venue was so full of people that I stopped to take it all in. I glanced around the room in amazement at the authors connecting with the community who showed up to chat with them. I didn't take a picture of that moment with my phone or camera, but it is seared in my memory because of the quiet joy that I

JOY, WHEN YOU ALLOW IT,
ONLY FEEDS MORE JOY.

experienced in that moment. I've tried to explain it to people, but I find myself at a loss for words because they don't seem to adequately express the beauty within that one snapshot of time.

———

Tonight, September 7th, after a full day of meetings, I secured a ticket for a Sunset Sound Bath experience at the last minute. I could feel the stress in my eyeballs and I noticed it in the way I responded to my spouse. I was trying to take it minute by minute like Michael McDonald said, but each minute that passed seemed to add just a smidge more stress to the metaphorical bucket I was carrying. I was as present as possible for check-ins, a virtual panel discussion, an interview with a local news station, and more. And as the time for the sound bath drew closer, that bucket of stress was full to the point that it had become hard to carry.

The second I parked my car, grabbed my yoga mat and headed towards the experience awaiting me on the lawn of the art museum, that bucket I had been carrying all day mysteriously disappeared. I set it down somewhere, but I'm still not sure where because I haven't found it yet. As I was laying on the mat, staring into the trees that seemed to smile down on me, I felt it again - that quiet joy had returned. I was prone, feet hanging slightly off the mat, connecting to the

ground below me, fingers caressing the grass beside me, thinking about all of my "Get Tos" - those things I feel lucky to get to do on a daily basis, and there it was. It wasn't a euphoric moment for me, but I inhaled deeply and exhaled a smile of contentment.

What I rediscovered in that moment was that the people in my circle and the work I get to do, all inspire joy - the one that's hanging out and waiting for permission to be seen, to poke its head out for a visit. When one person's light shines from within, we ourselves begin to glow, whether we know it or not. Similarly, joy - when you allow it, only feeds more joy. The key there is when we allow it. When we actively welcome joy in our lives, and not with an asterisk, that's when we keep the Joy Machine rolling. My joy is no different than your joy in that it's waiting for us to unleash it into the world to work its magic and move us to act in love. Let me clarify, it's not moving us to act like we're in love with someone, it moves us to create, to act, to change, to help with love at the core of our reason for acting.

In an old blog post from May of 2018, I wrote about the joy I witnessed on my Career Day tour.

Here is that entry:

> "The past few weeks have taken me on a Career Day tour to classrooms across the Kansas City Metropolitan area. I've had the chance to hang out

with some awesome students, share my Author/ Illustrator Origin Story with them, and hear more about what they're interested in doing for a living. Let me tell ya, the YouTubers are coming...I heard some really cool channel ideas and I hope they follow up on them!

What was exciting to see with each class rotation was

 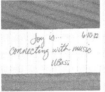 

the smile on the faces of each child as they entered the room ready to find out more about what I did, or the pride they showed as they shared their dream career with me. Each visit is a reminder of the source where joy and beauty originate.

Let me explain...

A Reflective Conversation

During this morning's Career Day presentation, I was waiting for a group of kids to get settled in on the rainbow rug when I noticed one student smiling at me from ear to ear. I greeted him with a nod since they were supposed to be getting into their listening positions. He began to nod in return while still smiling

JOY CAN LIVE WITHIN US, ABSENT OF ALL
THE THINGS WE FEAR.

wide and I could feel the words about to rise from his soul. I just wasn't entirely sure what he was going to say.

"You look happy!" he said to me.

"I am happy!" I replied in a whisper.

"You were smiling when we came in!" he continued.

"I was?" I asked in return.

I hadn't realized that I was smiling, but it didn't go unnoticed to him or any of the other students in this particular class. They all fell silent and with wide smiles, then nodded in excited agreement with this young man.

"It's so much fun to see how eager you all are to learn something new!" I said to the class aloud, no longer

whispering - since they were all paying attention.

What they didn't realize is that my smile was a reflection of the joy and beauty that their hearts brought into the room as they were so excited to hear about my career. Children are like walking and talking reminders of what we left behind (often because we

felt like we had to) along our journey into adulthood. While their hearts and souls are still pure, they radiate beauty."

That silent joy was hanging out within me even then, but I didn't know it at the depths at which I feel it now.

But what about…

Which one of you just allowed that thought in? I felt it. I'm

WE HAVE TO BE WILLING
TO GIVE OURSELVES SOME GRACE

not naming names, just know that I know you did it. Now that we've acknowledged that it happened, stop it. You could finish that statement with a thousand different possibilities.

But then what?

We fill the ether with whatabouts and a plethora of possibilities that we fear. Which wolf are you feeding; the fear or the freedom?

THE JOY MACHINE THRIVES
WHEN IT SENSES OUR OPEN NATURE

Sure, some of those things might happen. But what if they don't? If that was you who let that thought slip in just a few moments ago, hypothetically speaking, my guess is that you, like so many of us, have probably spent years and years waiting for the other shoe to drop. That doesn't mean things have to remain like that. Remember, if we're welcoming in joy, I mean truly welcoming it into our lives, we have to stay open to the possibility that joy can live within us absent of all the things we fear. To do this after years of conditioning ourselves to stave off disappointment, we have to be willing to give ourselves some grace. The Joy Machine thrives

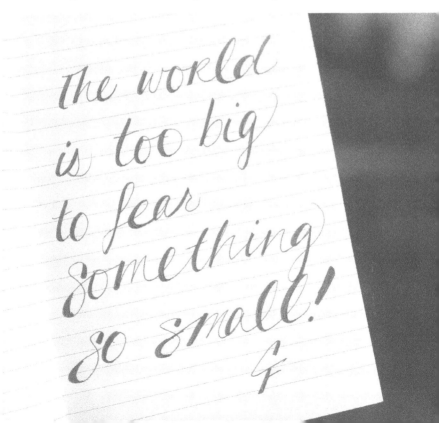

when it senses our open nature. Until we're there, our light will only flicker from time to time.

But guess what…

That flicker acts as a beacon that brings light workers our

THAT FLICKER OF LIGHT ACTS AS A BEACON THAT BRINGS LIGHT WORKERS OUR WAY

way, just when we need them the most. Your blinking light will begin to burn brighter and stronger with time, when you allow yourself to feel all versions of joy (yes, even the mouse whispers) without an asterisk.

Space and grace my friends. Space and grace.

CHAPTER SEVEN

TAKING STOCK OF WHAT IS

So I've been on this quest to find joy, and we know that it took me more than 20 years to get there - and *that* sounds ridiculous. I mean, think about what can happen in 20 years. If someone is born at the beginning of it, they can make it all the way through their K-12 experience and graduate from

UNLESS YOU HAVE A GOOD HANDLE ON WHO YOU ARE, AND WHAT DRIVES YOU, JOY IS LIKELY GOING TO FEEL A BIT ELUSIVE.

high school with two more years to go within the time that it took for me to find my joy. I know that's a little humorous. It's true though. But that 20 years wasn't stagnant growth. What was happening along the way, at least for me, is that I was taking stock of who I was. I was really stopping to consider what made me, me and what drove me as a person. And unless you have a good handle on who you are, and what drives you, joy is likely going to feel a bit elusive for you as

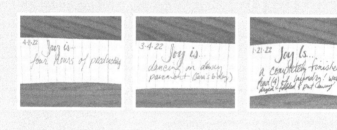

well. So in this chapter, this section, let's take stock of what it is.

Stop and reflect on the following questions. Really dig deep into the answer. Don't think about the surface level response that we give people on a regular basis. Think about what's really true for you at heart. These answers may stir up some responses that may not feel as positive as you'd like and that's okay, as long as you get to the core of who you are.

WHO ARE YOU TO YOU?

That's what matters most here.

The first question I was regularly answering along my (20-year) journey is, "Who are you?" That's a question I have been asked multiple times within the last two years, and I had honest answers ready to go because it was something that I had already given great consideration. Both coach and my therapist asked me at the beginning of our sessions,

THE CORE OF WHO YOU ARE IS THE START OF WHAT DRIVES YOU.

"Who are you?" They asked me to define it, not in terms of the work that I do, not in terms of who I am to other people, but who I am to myself. That's where you'll set a strong foundation for joy to thrive.

So, who are you to you?

What hats do you wear on a regular basis? Of those hats, which are your favorite? Which could you live with not wearing again? Now let's pause for just a second, why are you wearing those hats? Are those hats that you can get rid of or are those hats that you can give to someone else?

All right, let's continue. You figured out what hats you wear, which of those are your favorite, and which hats you could really live without wearing again, for whatever reason. But now let's stop and define your core values. What's most important to you of the list you see here?

INTEGRITY	IMPACT	CONNECTION	EXCEPTIONAL	RESPONSIBILITY
BOLDNESS	GENUINE	COURAGE	EMPATHY	PASSION
HONESTY	INNOVATION	RENEWAL	RESPECT	FUN
TRUST	STEWARDSHIP	BEAUTY	JUSTICE	CONTINUOUS LEARNING
ACCOUNTABILITY	PERFORMANCE	COST-CONSCIOUS	COLLABORATION	OWNERSHIP
CONSTANT IMPROVEMENT	LEADERSHIP	SUSTAINABILITY	INSPIRATION	COMMUNITY
CREATIVITY	QUALITY	SOCIAL VALUE	SIMPLICITY	VALUE
VALUE	TEAMWORK	TRUSTWORTHINESS	CONNECTION	INNOVATIVE

On the next page you'll find an exercise to complete. It's one that I usually use when I'm coaching people through identifying the core of their brand, whether that's their author brand, whether that is their brand as a person, whether that's their brand, as an organization. This is important because this is the core of who you are. This is the core of from where your actions grow. This is the beginning of what drives you.

As you look through the list of items on the preceding page, circle or at least identify - wait, maybe this isn't your book. Maybe this is a book that you borrowed from the library. *Definitely* don't circle it if this is a library book. If this is one that you borrowed from a friend, be kind. Give it back to them in the same manner in which you received it. If either of those are true, find a piece of paper. Write down your Top 10.

Great! Now that you've got your Top 10 written down, I want you to take that Top 10 and narrow it down to five.

Sometimes we can modify and shift our Top 10 through negotiation. Maybe there are two that are very similar or maybe there's one thing that's in your Top 10 that you must have in order to have the other item. Here's an example, say I've circled Honesty and Integrity. Maybe you believe to demonstrate integrity you have to demonstrate some sense of honesty. In this case, maybe that's the core of integrity, so I don't need both because it's implied that I'm honest if I live with integrity. Negotiate with yourself. See which values you're willing to give on. Identify which are non negotiable for you. Narrow that 10 down to five. Then, once you identify your five, I want you to - and I know, this might be painful for some of you. You can hate me now. Go ahead get it out. Process it. Feel those feelings. Curse me out. Do whatever you have to do. Say whatever you have to say, but then narrow the Top 5 down to three.

This is the core of who you are. This is the start of what drives you. Now here's my question, and this might sound

funny, but this is an opportunity for you to whittle down all of the extra hats and take those core values and really hone in on who you are.

If you were to describe yourself to someone in an elevator within 30 seconds, how would you do it? What would you say to them? How would you describe the essence of you?

Picture it, you get in an elevator with somebody famous or

somebody on their way to being famous. Maybe you're the somebody famous or maybe the somebody on their way to being famous. Whomever you're in the elevator with says, "Tell me about you." You can see in their eyes that they mean it. They're genuinely interested in learning more about you, but your floor is fast approaching.

DECODING JOY IS SO MUCH EASIER WHEN YOU HAVE A GREATER HANDLE ON WHO YOU ARE.

How would you describe yourself? What would you say?
Take a minute or two to write that down. Again, if this is a
borrowed book, *don't write it in the book.* Give it back to the
person the way that you found it. Write those ideas down on
that separate sheet of paper that you have.

By now you've figured out who you are, you've narrowed
down your values, you've narrowed down which hats are
your favorite and you've narrowed down how to describe
yourself to someone. If you haven't done all of these yet,
stop reading and come back to this paragraph when you're
done. If you don't, the water is about to get really muddy and
potentially overwhelming.

You good? Okay, let's talk about the work that you do in life.

What drives you?

Answer these questions:
Why do you do the work you do? Seriously, why do you do it? Whatever work you're doing in this moment right now. Outside of that work paying the bills, of all the career options available to you, why did you choose what you're currently doing?

 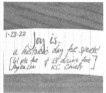 

If your answer to that question makes you feel a little sad or melancholy, answer this question. What would you do every day for free because you love it that much?

What feeling came over you when you read that last question? Giving away time is an interesting thing, right? We can't get time back. To my knowledge, they're not making anymore of it. Keeping that in mind, what is something that you love at your core so much that if someone asked for help in doing that thing, you would stop what you're doing to

WHAT DRIVES YOU?

teach them how to do it - without pay? This, is your passion.

Okay, so we've taken stock of who you are, your passion, and what drives you. And now my question is this; what do you really want out of life?

There are tons of commercials that attempt to help you define what you need. They tell you that you need this awesome thing in order to be productive. They tell you that

WHAT DO YOU NEED?

you need that trendy thing in order to be happy. Marketers are ingenious in that way. But really stop and think about whether or not you *need* some of those things that you believe are needs. Could they maybe fall into a want instead?

What do you want?

What do you need?

And, what are your wildest dreams?

That's it, kind of. Answer those questions so you can start to take stock of *what is*, for yourself, then finish the following statement and answer the final 3 questions:

- My purpose is to…(insert your top 3 values here)
- Who am I? What do I do? Why do I do it? (insert your favorite hats and your why here)

Decoding joy is so much easier when you have a greater handle on who you are, what brings you happiness and hope, and where you can start to find and create your own joy.

WHERE CAN YOU START TO
CREATE MORE JOY?

CHAPTER EIGHT

MANIFESTING JOY

Define it for yourself. Be specific. Speak it into existence. Nurture it.

I was talking to a friend the other day about how joy works. It was pretty perplexing to have this conversation and step outside of myself in thinking about joy and how it has shown up in my life.

OFTEN, JOY SEEMS LIKE
SUCH AN ELUSIVE THING.

In talking about manifesting and finding ways to invite joy in, I had a definitive answer. It surprised me that I had an answer so strong and so direct about how joy works. Often joy seems like such an elusive thing.

The truth is that joy is pretty simple. Joy shows up where it's welcome. Joy shows up where it's invited. Just like us (well most of us anyway), we show up where we're welcome.

We show up where we're invited. And if the vibe is off, we usually don't stay. Sometimes we don't even go. Joy is the same way. If you choose to welcome joy in your life. You have to be willing to create an environment that encourages joy to stay. If you choose to welcome joy in your life you have to set the vibe that allows joy to feel welcome. Otherwise, it will leave - and sometimes it won't show up because we're not ready for it.

JOY SHOWS UP WHERE IT'S WELCOME.

So when we're talking about how joy works, we have to make sure that we're working as well. Joy is not something that happens to us, joy is something that we foster, and create, and work with, to create more of. Joy doesn't exist in a vacuum. Joy feeds and thrives off of more joy being present. Joy lives on moments that exist in quiet and in still, and even the big boisterous moments.

But the common thread that ties those various times together is the gratitude we show for the joy that exists.

JOY DOESN'T EXIST IN A VACUUM.

Imagine if this were you, someone invited you in, welcomed you, created an environment that was comfortable, and then didn't express any interest in your presence or that you chose to visit them when you could've been elsewhere. You might hang out for a bit, but returning is another story entirely. Gratitude is the often spoken of variable that exists, but its value definitely feels underrated.

It's tremendously important for us to demonstrate our gratitude for the presence of joy in some shape or form, if for no other reason than we want it to return. Okay. So how do we manifest it already?

When it comes to manifesting joy it really is as simple as these three steps:

1. **DEFINE JOY FOR YOURSELF -** You've heard what it means to me, and I'm sure to others. Sometimes people may have even tried to tell you what your joy isn't. That's not their business. It's yours. What is joy to you? What does joy feel like to you? How does joy show up for you? Define it for yourself so you can recognize it when it's present. Be specific.

2. **BE PREPARED** - I mean well prepared, to invite joy in for a visit. Tend to the dust, vacuum the floor, stack the magazines up, throw the trash away. You don't have to wipe down the baseboards, but tidy up your internal space so joy feels welcome. Create a hope-filled place for it to hang out and thrive. Remember, joy multiplies like Gremlins in water to create more of itself.

 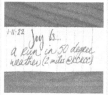 

3. **NURTURE IT** - Be grateful for the joy that shows up. Make sure that you're willing to acknowledge what joy has poured into your life and then actually acknowledge it. That acknowledgement can be verbal. It can be written and it can also be in how we choose to live our lives.

Here's one of the many ways I've expressed gratitude for the joy that I'm nurturing. I started posting silly videos of

WHEN WE ARE VULNERABLE ENOUGH TO SHARE OUR JOY WITH OTHERS, IT ONLY SERVES TO INVITE MORE JOY INTO EVERYONE'S LIFE.

myself on Instagram and on Facebook (in 2022) of some of the more quiet moments in my life where I'm just heating up a bowl of oatmeal. Sounds boring and drab right? Nobody wants to see a video of me standing there watching the microwave. I almost dozed just thinking about how long that two minutes would feel. Sounds like a snoozefest, right? It's definitely the opposite.

Because of the joy that exists in my life, the joy that I have invited in, the joy that I nurture, all of it bubbles up into a

WHEN WE SHARE OUR JOY OUTWARDLY,
OTHERS BEGIN TO TAKE NOTICE OF IT.

variety of outward expressions for me. Sometimes it shows up as me singing random songs through the house about something that I observe. And sometimes it's as simple as these videos I started posting; literally waiting for my oatmeal to finish heating up in the microwave and dancing to some random song because that's what I was feeling in the moment. Dancing while waiting for your oatmeal sounds a tad bit more interesting maybe, yes?

What has been the most interesting piece for me in sharing

these videos are the responses that I have received from people. I'm not even sure why I was compelled to post the first one in the first place, other than a moment of, "Hey, this is a more human side of me the writer, the author, the speaker, the business owner." I'm a little quirky so I posted it, but the number of people who have commented either on the video or when they see me in person, about how those videos bring them joy because they can see the joy

on my face - that has been the most surprising part by far. I love, love, love hearing that type of feedback from people. It encourages me to find other ways to outwardly express the joy that I feel inside. Then what's happening is twofold.

One, not only do I get to experience more joy, but also - two, I'm encouraging others to go out and find their joy. Not find it and hold on to it in a quiet way, but to go out and share their joy with other people as well. What happens when we start to share that joy outwardly? Other people take notice of it. They start to feel something very similar. It encourages and inspires people to seek out their own unique joy. Remember, the Joy Machine keeps rolling when we're open.

To manifest joy, we have to first create a space where we wholly and hopefully welcome it. Then create a space where we nurture it, and also be willing to create a space where we are vulnerable enough to share that joy with others in an outward expression. Because then, it only serves to invite more joy into everyone's life.

You don't want to be a joy hoarder. That doesn't create an environment where joy wants to hang out and stay. Joy multiplies - rapidly. There's enough for everyone. Share it wide and share it freely.

See? Simple, in theory. But it is a practice. Go manifest some joy and help others invite it into their lives as well.

DON'T BE A JOY HOARDER.

CHAPTER NINE

NOW WHAT?

Have you ever had the chance to fly on a rainy day? One of the best reminders of life's promise can be found just after takeoff. On the ground, it's gloomy and moody, but once you crest the clouds, the sun shows its bright face. It's so easy for us to forget that the sun still shines when it's completely obscured by dense clouds. The same is true of just about anything in our lives.

WITH ONE STEP AT A TIME
WE'LL FIND OUR WAY BACK
TO THE WARMTH AND JOY OF THE SUN.

So how do we find that sliver of sun when all around us seems to be gloomy?

We have to hold near to us, the memory of the sun and recall that visual of a plane ascending above the clouds. With one foot in front of the other, one literal step at a time, we'll find our way back to the warmth and joy of the sun and the promise of brighter days.

 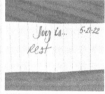 

Likewise, we have the choice of how readily we keep joy in our lives. On those days that aren't as enjoyable as others, we can choose to hold onto the memory of more joyous occasions while still feelings all the things that accompany the stress or strife that's in front of us in the moment. It is in these moments that we strengthen our ability to actively conjure up or manifest the type of joy that we want in our lives.

"WE HAVE A CHOICE OF HOW READILY WE KEEP JOY IN OUR LIVES."

Each of us has the power to keep it near or let it lapse into near non-existence. You get to select which option you want to nurture at any given moment, and choosing one now doesn't mean you can't choose something different later. That's the beauty of the human mind.

But, if you want joy to reside with you for longer spells, if you want it to be a permanent houseguest hanging out in the mother-in-law suite of your soul, that's something you have the power to create through consistent action. Make joy and

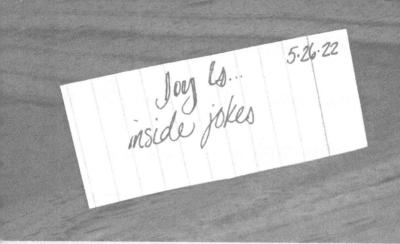

Joy is...
inside jokes

5.26.22

MAKE JOY AND YOUR PURSUIT OF IT A HABIT.

your pursuit of it a habit.

The Joy Challenge awaits as a spark to get you moving. One week. Seven days in a row. Document in photos or in words, what brings you joy. I can't wait to see what you invite in.

Now I know you were taught along the way that sharing is caring. Don't hoard your decoded knowledge. Don't limit the addition of joy to just your life. Bring others along on this joy journey with you. Let them borrow your copy of the book - unless you wrote in it, then gift them a copy of their own. Invite others to community conversations about their joy journey. Tag them in on join your Joy Challenge - invite someone new to join you each day. Create your own ripples of joy.

And, if you're in search of some additional resources, check out decodingjoy.co

CREATE YOUR OWN RIPPLES OF JOY.

BONUS

JOYSPIRATION

The next few pages are filled with joyspiration, more moments of joy that filled my joy-jar from the first half of this year. If you're ready to move beyond the Joy Challenge and welcome joy in your life on a daily basis, a joy jar or journal is a good way to go.

I absolutely LOVE the visual aspect of a clear glass jar that allows me to see that there's at least a handful of things for me to be grateful for. A joy jar, though, only allows for so much space on your entries. A journal expands your opportunity to add details surrounding your joy.

WELCOME JOY IN YOUR LIFE
ON A DAILY BASIS.

"I WOKE UP ONE DAY AND REALIZED I WAS GIVING MY JOY AWAY TO OTHERS AND NOT KEEPING ANY..."

FINDING JOY DURING OVERWHELM MIGHT SEEM
LIKE A PIPE DREAM.

"JOY IS A DEEP-ROOTED HAPPINESS THAT'S HANGING OUT BEHIND ALL WE'VE CRAMMED IN FRONT OF IT."

TO KNOW JOY THERE MUST BE AN
APPRECIATION FOR THE BALANCE IN WHICH IT
CAN EXIST.

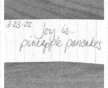

"WHEN WE HOLD SPACE FOR EACH OTHER,
WE ARE HELPING TO FOSTER JOY."

JOY IS SOMETHING MUCH DEEPER THAN HAPPINESS.

"JOY REQUIRES SURRENDER IN ORDER TO EXPERIENCE ITS FULLNESS."

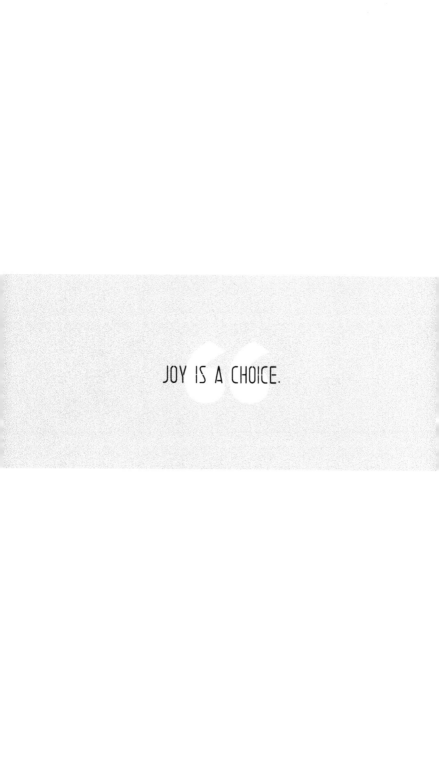

JOY IS A CHOICE.

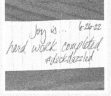

"IMPOSTER SYNDROME SHOWED OUT WHEN IT
SHOWED UP."

THE REASON I KNOW JOY SO WELL IS
BECAUSE I ALSO KNOW SADNESS.

"BECAUSE I ALLOW IT TO DO ITS WORK WITHIN ME, I'M TRULY ABLE TO APPRECIATE WHEN THINGS ARE JOYOUS."

I DON'T WALK AROUND HAPPY ALL THE TIME,
BUT I STILL KNOW DEEP JOY.

"GLIMPSES OF JOY AREN'T ENOUGH TO SATIATE THE SPIRIT."

I FOUND MYSELF CLOSER TO JOY, BUT NOT
QUITE THERE YET.

"I PLOPPED MY EMOTIONAL FLOTATION DEVICES ONTO MY ARMS AND RELAXED INTO THE WAVES OF CHANGE."

THAT WAS WHEN I BEGAN TO FEEL A DEEPER LEVEL OF HOPE.

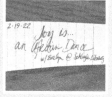

"JOY ISN'T ALWAYS A FEELING OF
EUPHORIA."

JOY SOMETIMES SLIPS IN DURING QUIET
MOMENTS AND FILLS YOUR SOUL WITH LIGHT.

"JOY, WHEN YOU ALLOW IT,
ONLY FEEDS MORE JOY."

JOY CAN LIVE WITHIN US, ABSENT OF ALL
THE THINGS WE FEAR.

"UNLESS YOU HAVE A GOOD HANDLE ON WHO YOU ARE, AND WHAT DRIVES YOU, JOY IS LIKELY GOING TO FEEL A BIT ELUSIVE."

THE CORE OF WHO YOU ARE IS THE START
OF WHAT DRIVES YOU.

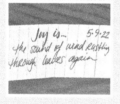

"DECODING JOY IS SO MUCH EASIER WHEN YOU HAVE A GREATER HANDLE ON WHO YOU ARE."

OFTEN, JOY SEEMS LIKE
SUCH AN ELUSIVE THING.

"JOY SHOWS UP WHERE IT'S WELCOME."

JOY DOESN'T EXIST IN A VACUUM.

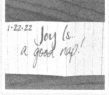

"WHEN WE ARE VULNERABLE ENOUGH
TO SHARE OUR JOY WITH OTHERS, IT
ONLY SERVES TO INVITE MORE JOY INTO
EVERYONE'S LIFE."

WITH ONE STEP AT A TIME WE'LL FIND OUR WAY BACK TO THE WARMTH AND JOY OF THE SUN.

  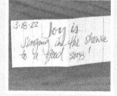

"WE HAVE A CHOICE OF HOW READILY WE KEEP JOY IN OUR LIVES."

MAKE JOY AND YOUR PURSUIT OF IT A
HABIT.

"CREATE YOUR OWN RIPPLES OF JOY."

DON'T BE A JOY HOARDER. SPREAD THE WORD.

A3Jul ThE AuThJR

By day, C. L. Fails is the Founder & CEO of LaunchCrate Publishing - a company created to help writers launch their work into the world while retaining the portion of profit they deserve.

By night, C. L. is a multi-genre author and illustrator for several book series. Additionally, she is an accidental educator, having served pre-school through college students in her hometown of Kansas City. Always an agent for equity, she has dedicated her career to helping others learn to follow their internal compass, and thrive despite challenge.

When she's not working on a book, leading a workshop, making music, or baking, you can find her doodling on whatever object may be nearby.

Want to learn more? Scan the code.

CPSIA information can be obtained
at www.ICGtesting.com
Printed in the USA
JSHW022322031222
34065JS00005B/7/J